Weird and Wacky
INVENTIONS

BY JIM MURPHY

SKY PONY PRESS • NEW YORK

The first is for Kyran Murphy

Sky Pony Press books may be purchased in bulk at special discounts for sales promotion, corporate gifts, fund-raising, or educational purposes. Special editions can also be created to specifications. For details, contact the Special Sales Department, Sky Pony Press, 307 West 36th Street, 11th Floor, New York, NY 10018 or info@skyhorsepublishing.com.

Sky Pony® is a registered trademark of Skyhorse Publishing, Inc.®, a Delaware corporation.

Visit our website at www.skyponypress.com.

10 9 8 7 6 5 4 3 2 1

Manufactured in China, October 2015
This product conforms to CPSIA 2008

Library of Congress Cataloging-in-Publication Data is available on file.

Cover design by Brian Peterson

Paperback ISBN: 978-1-63450-203-0
Ebook ISBN: 978-1-62636-586-5

Contents

Introduction

One day in 1849, Walter Hunt began tinkering with a piece of wire. Hunt was trying to invent an improved type of rifle for the army. One of the things he needed for his rifle was a small wire clasp that could be opened and closed many times without breaking. He also wanted it to have a spring so that it would open easily. After three hours of twisting and bending the wire, Hunt created something he didn't expect. Instead of a clasp to be attached to a rifle, he invented what turned out to be one of the world's greatest little gadgets—the safety pin.

We all know what a safety pin looks like. Very few of us, however, think of such a common, everyday item as having been invented, let alone wonder who invented it. Look around the room you're in and you'll discover hundreds of things that did not exist before someone like Walter Hunt created them. In fact, just about everything you see or use has been invented: cars, faucets, nails, many types of flowers and plants, refrigerators, televisions, stereos, pens, hamburgers, and the catsup that goes on top.

Since its founding in 1790, the United States Patent and Trademark Office has issued over 4 million patents for inventions of every conceivable kind. Our history books tell us about the most famous inventors, people like Benjamin Franklin, Eli Whitney, Cyrus McCormick, Charles Goodyear, Alexander Graham Bell, George Eastman, and Thomas Edison, to name just a few. Yet a surprising number of inventions were created by people who did not spend their working day in laboratories fiddling with metal, wood, and chemicals. Many of America's inventors were carpenters and mechanics, shopkeepers, artists, teachers, factory and office workers—ordinary people who simply had an idea they thought would be of some benefit to the general populace.

After these people had thought out their concept as much as they could, and maybe even made a working model of it, they applied to the Patent and Trademark Office for a patent. The general procedure for getting a patent is described at the back of this book; part of the procedure is to supply a drawing of the invention.

What follows is a good-natured quiz involving the patent drawings of some of the lesser-known inventors. Each of the drawings has a clue that hints, sometimes directly, sometimes indirectly, at what the inventions were supposed to do. A number of possible answers accompany the drawing and help you in your guessing.

As you turn the pages, you'll be surprised to discover the many kinds of things that were thought up over the years. Some of them were truly ahead of their time, interesting concepts but too complicated or not efficient enough to operate or manufacture. A few were useful in their time but seem very old-fashioned or quaint to us today. And just about all of them are now considered rather odd, or silly, or, as the title says, weird and wacky.

But we shouldn't judge these inventions too harshly. After all, the things we consider modern now will begin to look strange as new things are invented to replace or improve on them. What is more, each one of the inventions you will see, no matter how outlandish, represents an individual's attempt to come to grips with, duplicate, and in some cases overcome the forces of nature. Each is a step, sometimes a very tiny step, toward making things a little better or faster or more long-lasting. Above all, they are a tribute to the creative spirit that will work long into the night, overcome financial and educational obstacles, and endure ridicule in order to turn a dream into a reality.

From the Neck Up

Each morning we go through a ritual of studying our own sleepy faces in the mirror, brushing our teeth, and combing our hair. Some people will shave, others will put on makeup. Before we go out, we give ourselves a final check to be sure the part of us that sits on our shoulders looks as good as it can.

Inventors have given a lot of thought to the area from our neck up. See if you can figure out what they had in mind when they invented the following things.

This machine had many gears and springs. It was supposed to be attached to something else, and when the metal arm and ball at the left moved forward, the apparatus went into operation. The invention would make any meeting with the user a polite encounter.

1. a head-measuring device
2. an automatic tipping-hat
3. a hat-and-head cooler
4. a machine to stimulate the brain

TIPPING-HAT In 1896 James Boyle decided the world needed an automatic tipping-hat. The mechanism was first wound up like an alarm clock and then fastened to whichever hat was to be worn that day. Next the wearer put the hat on his head, and a number of curved-spring "fingers" firmly secured both the hat and the machinery in place.

Once the hat was on the head, operating it was simple. The gentleman bowed his head slightly and the arm and ball pendulum shifted forward, triggering the machinery into action. To the amazement of passersby, the hat would tip itself, swing around in a complete circle, and gently settle back into place. If the wearer had an armful of packages, this invention made it simple for him to tip his hat. And the wearer's hair wouldn't even be mussed up. What could be more polite!

Because hats were once worn by so many people, from businessmen to shopkeepers to stagecoach drivers to cooks, inventors lavished much attention on devices for the hat, since their inventions, if accepted, would be sold to thousands and thousands of people. To ensure that a hat fit perfectly, complicated instruments were devised to measure the size and contours of the head. In addition, hats came to be used as hearing aids, spying implements, and, to provide comfort during the summer, there were special *hat ventilators* to cool the wearer's head. The one on the left was invented in 1860 by James Jenkinson, the one on the right by Albert Lee Eliel in 1890. Both of these hat ventilators were operated in the same way. A wind-up mechanism, much like the one that ran the tipping-hat, spun a tiny fan that was attached to the inside of the hat.

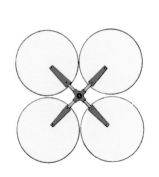

The user of this 1924 invention held the long handle portion at the right in one hand. An electric motor inside the handle turned the larger wheel. As complicated as this drawing may appear, the inventor hoped his invention would make a daily procedure cut and dried.

1. a scalp shampooer and massager
2. a wrinkle remover
3. an eye-examining device
4. an electric safety razor

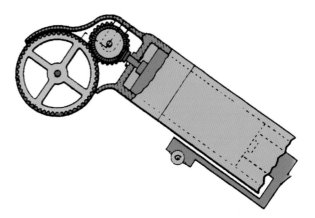

This 1961 invention was made of rubber and was operated by hand.

1. a hairbrush for horses and sheep
2. a mustache curler
3. a facial scrubber
4. a toothbrush for dogs and cats

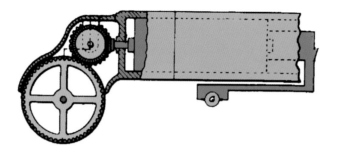

ELECTRIC SAFETY RAZOR

ELECTRIC SAFETY RAZOR This is an early electric safety razor invented by Charles Bailey. The sharp cutting blades were built into the large wheel. As this large wheel turned, the user would move it back and forth across his face, cutting facial hair in the process. The interesting thing about this razor is that the blades came into direct contact with the skin. So while this was obviously a faster way to shave, it increased the chances of cuts and nicks and could hardly be considered a "safety" razor. Now most electric razors have a fine mesh screen that separates the blades from the skin, reducing the possibility of accidents.

TOOTHBRUSH FOR DOGS AND CATS Even dogs and cats need to have their teeth cleaned, so Bird Eyer invented this toothbrush for dogs and cats. It is used just like an ordinary toothbrush. The up-and-down and back-and-forth movement of the soft spikes and cylinders was supposed to remove food particles and any tartar buildup. While this sounds very simple to do, in practice it is not. Dogs and cats have very sensitive gums, so even the most careful brushing is painful. Today most people take their dog or cat to the veterinarian to have its teeth cleaned. There the animal is given a mild anesthetic to eliminate the pain, and an electric machine just like the one that cleans our teeth is used.

This invention consisted of a hat made of a hard material and a streamer made of a flexible fabric. When the streamer moved, the wearer was supposed to enjoy what happened.

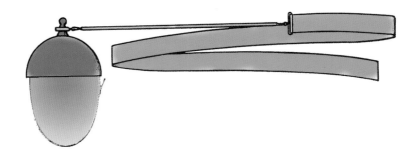

1. a toy hat
2. an army helmet with portable weather detector
3. a motorcycle helmet, radio, and advertising banner
4. a rain hat and lightning rod

Carl Wahl wanted his machine to make an important activity that we do every day easier and more efficient. The handle on one end turned a small, soft brush at the other end.

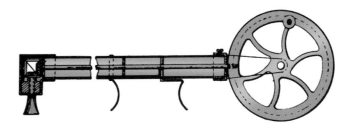

1. an applicator for cosmetics
2. a shoe polisher
3. a tooth-cleaning device
4. a device for cleaning glasses

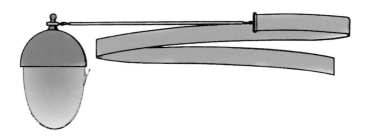

TOY HAT This is a toy hat patented in 1966. As the illustration shows, the hat was placed on the head and held there by a strap. The wearer would then move his or her head in a circle, causing the streamer to whirl in pretty patterns. The possibility of getting hit in the eye by the streamer may have been one reason this invention did not become popular. Moreover, by spinning the head around so much, the wearer could develop a severe headache.

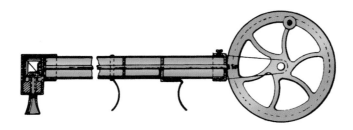

TOOTH-CLEANING DEVICE If you turned the handle on Carl Wahl's 1930 tooth-cleaning device fast enough and long enough, it was supposed to do a better job than the standard toothbrush. The user held the two wires at the bottom of the device between the thumb and the index finger. The small end went into the mouth and had a soft brush that spun around when the handle was turned. However, Mr. Wahl's invention was much too complicated and cumbersome, and the ordinary toothbrush is still used today.

This contraption looks odder than it really was. It used air and heat to make short work of an activity that people had to have done every so often.

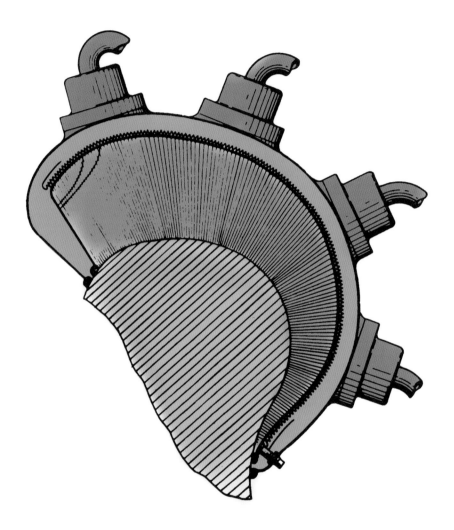

1. a space helmet
2. a vacuum device for relieving headaches
3. a hair-cutting machine
4. a stimulator for hair growth

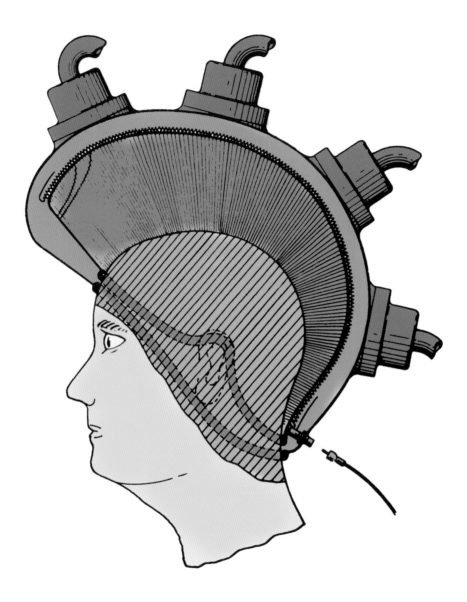

HAIR-CUTTING MACHINE John Boax's 1951 hair-cutting machine used an air exhaust system to suck hair straight up into tiny holes where electric coils would instantly burn the hair to the desired length. Mr. Boax realized that everyone has special preferences in the way their hair is cut, and he suggested that "a set of masks of various sizes and shapes be provided to suit different sizes and shapes of heads as well as to provide for different lengths of hair." Unfortunately for Mr. Boax, there was too much chance that his invention would seriously burn the hair, so hand scissors are still used to cut hair today.

Believe it or not, this simple wire clip helped to solve a particularly troublesome social problem of the late nineteenth century.

1. a collar-and-tie fastener
2. a mustache guard
3. a way to secure ears under hats
4. a bobby pin

Martin Goetze of Berlin, Germany, was granted a U.S. patent on this implement in 1896. With it he left his mark everywhere.

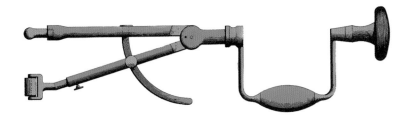

1. an ear cleaner
2. a dentist's cavity packer
3. a compass for measuring head size
4. a dimple maker

MUSTACHE GUARD With big, bushy mustaches very much in fashion, something had to be done to keep food from being caught in them. So Charles Miller invented a mustache guard in 1882. The wearer needed two of them, one for each side of his mustache.

When the clips were inserted into the mustache, they gathered the little hairs into a neat bundle. As silly as this invention might seem, keeping mustaches clean was a major concern to men of this era. Over twenty patents were granted for various kinds of mustache guards. In 1876, V. A. Gates patented this cloth guard. It was tied around the ears, and the cloth shield hid and protected the mustache. Twenty years later, in 1896, J. Dal invented these large clips that worked like spring-action clothespins.

DIMPLE MAKER Whenever something is in vogue, inventors often think up gadgets related to it. And so, during a time when dimples were considered especially attractive, Goetze invented this dimple maker. It is operated like a hand drill. The rounded knob (made of ivory, marble, Celluloid, or rubber) is placed on the site of the future dimple and the roller is rotated around and around by turning the handle. If nothing more permanent or damaging results, a dimple will appear and last for six or eight hours.

Something to Wear

When we talk about things to wear, we usually think of clothes—suits, dresses, shoes, for instance. The following section contains inventions that were worn by the user. Sometimes they looked like ordinary clothes or shoes; sometimes they were simply strapped onto some area of the body. However they were worn, each one had a special use. See how many you can guess.

These shoes and head gear were simple to store away and could be buckled on whenever there was an emergency. Benjamin Oppenheimer hoped his 1879 invention would result in sure-fire sales.

1. a fire escape
2. an umbrella and galoshes
3. a sunshade and sandals
4. a protective garment for construction workers

FIRE ESCAPE With buildings getting taller and taller in the second half of the last century, Mr. Oppenheimer felt this was the only logical kind of fire escape. While the fire raged below, an individual would calmly put on the hat-parachute device and the padded shoes. Once the user had jumped from a window or off the roof, the parachute would carry him safely past the flames, and the shoes would ensure a gentle landing. Unfortunately, the inventor said nothing about the difficulty of buckling straps as a fire rushed closer, or the possibility that the wind might carry the jumper toward the burning building, or the distinct chance that the chin buckle could choke the user in flight.

O nce the users buckled this odd-looking device on, the inventor insisted that they would have a new view of things.

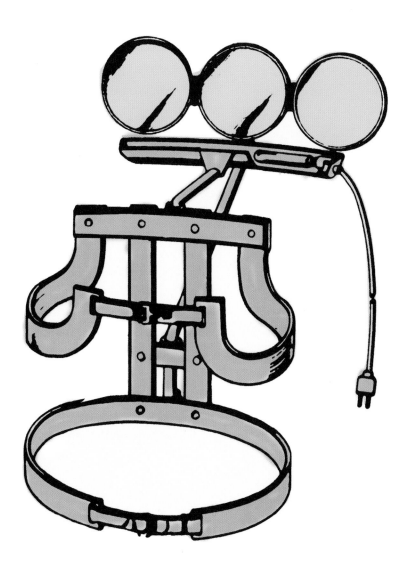

1. a corrective back brace
2. a jet harness for short, low-altitude flights
3. a telescopic camera
4. a back mirror

BACK MIRROR An ordinary mirror will let a person see the front, top, and sides of the head but would never show the back. In order to provide a full view, Edward O'Brien invented this back mirror in 1952. The wearer slipped it on like a jacket and plugged in the mirror light for extra illumination. By facing a large mirror, the user could see a reflection of the hair on the back of the head in the three round mirrors.

Almost fifty years earlier, in 1905, Emmie Alice Thayer and Emily Waitee Thayer patented a *wearable mirror* that attempted to solve the same problem. Back then, many people faced a wall mirror and used a hand mirror to see the top and back of the head and body. This meant that only one hand was free to comb the hair or straighten a hat. When the mirror was worn like a pair of glasses, both hands were freed and the user had a clear view of "the topmost feather on her hat, her collar or even her skirt."

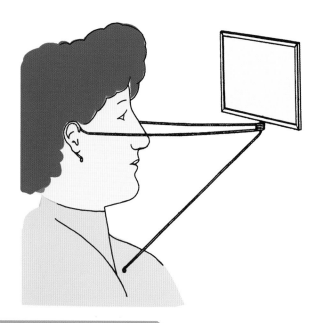

This 1965 invention was worn on the arm.

1. a reusable cast
2. an arm-and-hand purse
3. a waterproof carrying case for newspapers and magazines
4. a portable arm radio

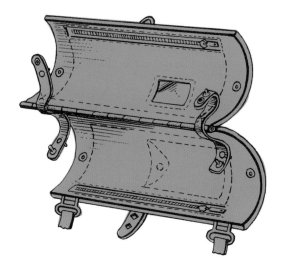

This 1973 invention could be made out of metal or hard plastic and was intended to be worn in the hot summer sunlight.

1. a pair of telescopic glasses
2. a sunbather's toe-rings
3. an eyeglass camera
4. a pair of sunglasses for observing eclipses

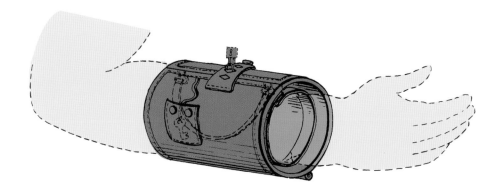

ARM-AND-HAND PURSE Robert Todd's arm-and-hand purse might not be elegant enough for formal occasions, but its other functions made it very useful. Because it was always attached to the arm, the wearer would never leave it somewhere by mistake. Also, it could be locked, which made it very difficult for a purse snatcher to steal. Finally, there was a strap that converted it into a hand purse.

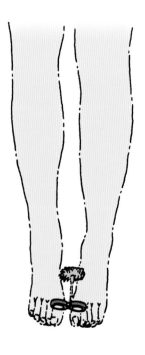

SUNBATHER'S TOE-RINGS Russell Greathouse was so worried that people were getting uneven tans that he devised these sunbather's toe-rings. They were put on each big toe to prevent the feet from naturally spreading apart when the user was stretched out on the beach. The result would be an even tan. Mr. Greathouse provided a tiny hole in the center for a flower (plastic or real) for the user's viewing pleasure.

Frances Allen's 1972 patent wasn't supposed to be good-looking, but it was meant to improve the way a person looked and felt.

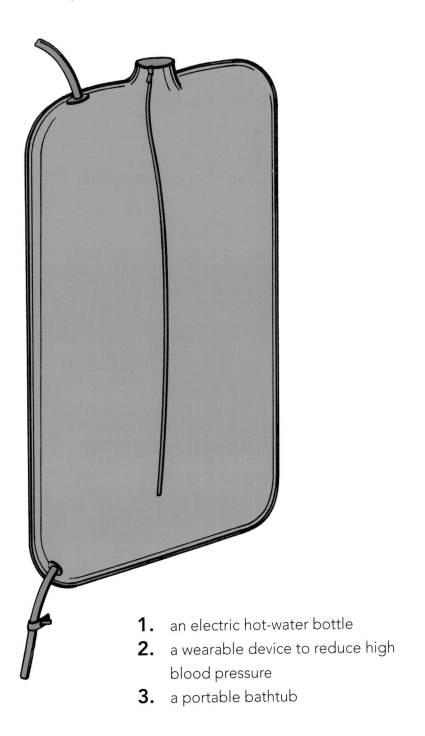

1. an electric hot-water bottle
2. a wearable device to reduce high blood pressure
3. a portable bathtub

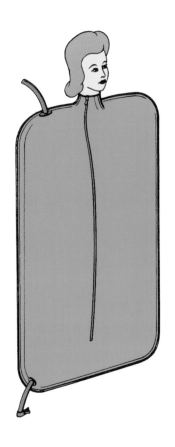

PORTABLE BATHTUB After a long, dusty journey, Frances Allen hoped her portable bathtub would relax and restore the spirits of any traveler. All the user had to do was attach the hoses to a water source and a drain and step in. The person could close the bag with a zipper on the inside and begin to scrub away. Once the bath was over, the plastic bag was drained, and rolled up for another day's traveling.

As odd as this may seem, many people have invented portable bathtubs over the years. One reason for this was that the quality of hotels and their bathing facilities varied a great deal from area to area. In 1904, Adolf Herz patented the *portable bath* pictured below. It was actually very similar to Frances Allen's invention. The major difference was that the water was placed in the bottom of Herz's model before the user stepped into it.

Half-Baked Helpers

Because the preparing, serving, and preservation of food are so important to all of us, inventors have found this area a rich source of inspiration. All kinds of helpful gadgets have been created, from refrigerators to microwave ovens to waffle makers. This section contains inventions that never became household items.

William Lance's 1866 patent was supposed to be used in restaurants and cafeterias. It was run by gears hidden below the surface and was meant to save time and space.

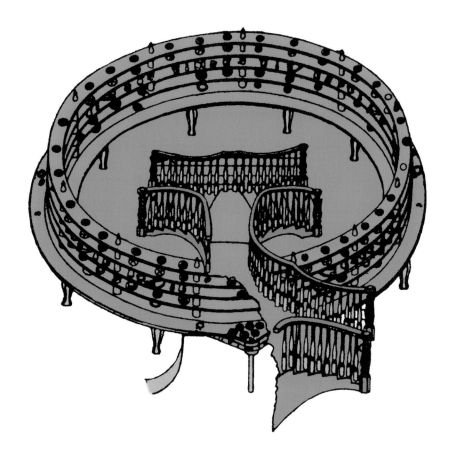

1. an automatic dishwasher
2. an oven for preparing banquets
3. a self-waiting table

SELF-WAITING TABLE William Lance's self-waiting table had a series of driving gears concealed underneath it. These allowed the five serving shelves to revolve in a counterclockwise direction while the eating counter remained in one place. The table had a staircase (partially shown) that gave access to the center of the giant table. The diner would simply pull up a chair and pick the most appealing dishes as they went by on the shelves. Because the number of people living and working in cities increased greatly during the nineteenth century, restaurants were required to speedily serve more and more customers, especially at lunchtime. Lance's self-waiting table was one answer to the call for increased seating and serving efficiency.

The front of this was made of clear glass and, when put on properly, it would act as a protective covering.

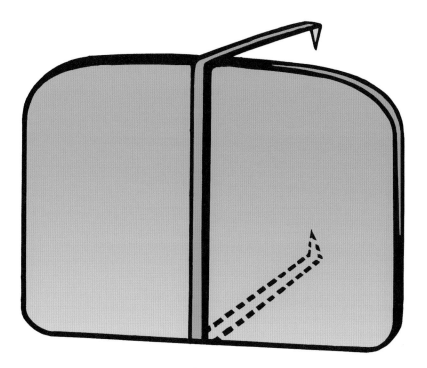

1. a cook's antisplatter goggles
2. a bread preserver
3. a cover for boiling pots
4. an oven door

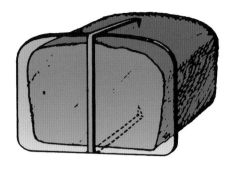

BREAD PRESERVER Wilhelm Biber had this bread preserver patented in 1905. The glass plate was placed firmly against a freshly cut loaf of bread and the hooks held the plate in place.

Shielding the cut end from the air retained moisture, so that the bread wouldn't get hard so quickly. Other similar devices included J. Black's 1875 *cheese preserver* and James Harrell's 1952 *pie preserver*. These were all interesting ideas, but none of them became household necessities. For one thing, each required that the bread, cheese, or pie be cut precisely to the shape of the invention. While all of the inventions were made to fit pieces of various sizes, they couldn't seal the irregular wedges and ends that most people cut. Now plastic wrap fits and seals even the oddest shapes.

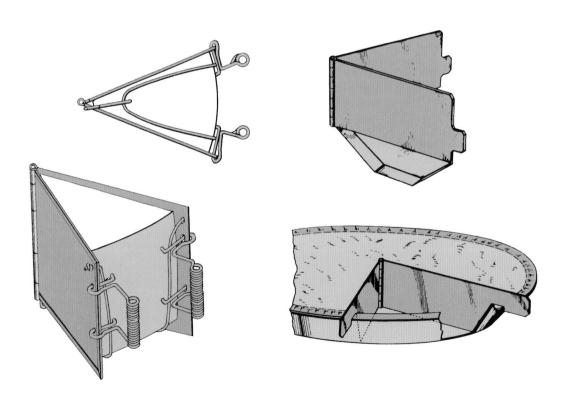

Open wide for a big surprise. This is obviously a spoon, but for what?

1. a measuring spoon
2. a combination spoon and straw
3. a spoon for watering houseplants
4. a medicine spoon
5. a soup spoon

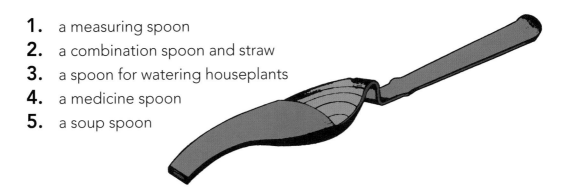

This 1897 patent was made of sheet metal and had movable parts. Its first use was as a *container for grocery goods*, but it could do something else as well.

1. a slicer
2. a mousetrap
3. a grater and shredder
4. a fly trap

MEDICINE SPOON This medicine spoon, patented in 1906, was designed by William Jerkins to ensure that every drop of medicine was swallowed. The inventor stressed that it could be used to administer medicine to humans and animals, thereby increasing its sales potential. As with forks and other everyday utensils, many variations were invented to provide the utmost comfort and usefulness. C. Sanford's 1952 *spoon with base* made it possible to measure out the right quantity of liquid or solid for a recipe beforehand and set it safely aside until needed.

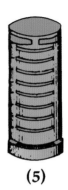

ALL FOUR CHOICES Robert Gardiner worked and worked to develop many possible uses for his gadget. It began as a *container for grocery goods* (Fig. 1) with a removable top. It could also be used as a *grater and shredder* (Fig. 2) with tiny cutting holes, or as a *slicer* (Fig. 3). When placed on its side, with a small screen inserted, it became a *mousetrap* (Fig. 4) that allowed the mouse to enter but not leave. When left upright, it became a *fly trap* (Fig. 5). With five different uses, Gardiner's invention was a real bargain.

(1)

(2)

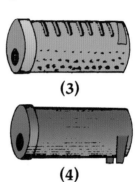

(3)

(4)

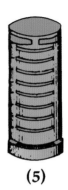

(5)

This is not a pitchfork for pitching hay. It is a fork invented in 1975 to be used for one kind of food.

1. a salad fork
2. a spaghetti fork
3. a mixed vegetables fork
4. a french-fried potato fork

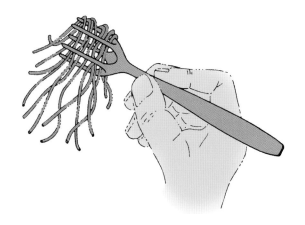

SPAGHETTI FORK While it might work for any of these foods, Malcolm Braid intended this to be used as a spaghetti fork. The fork had five prongs set widely apart and the base of the fork was not flat. Instead the prongs were at different levels. This design enabled the fork to hold more spaghetti than an ordinary one. Below are a few other specially designed forks. The first is a *vegetable fork* patented in 1895 by George Dow. It was intended to help lift and serve boiled potatoes, carrots, turnips, and cabbage. Once the vegetable had been speared, the user squeezed the handles together and the bar connecting the handle and two prongs slid forward, pushing the hot vegetable onto the dish. The second object is a *combination fork, egg beater, and dish lifter* invented in 1907 by H. J. Vasconcelles. One end was a fork, but its rounded handle could be used to beat eggs and to lift a hot dish by its edge.

This invention was made from thin sheet metal and could be fastened on very easily by tiny sharp needles. Once in position, it prevented early morning accidents at the kitchen table.

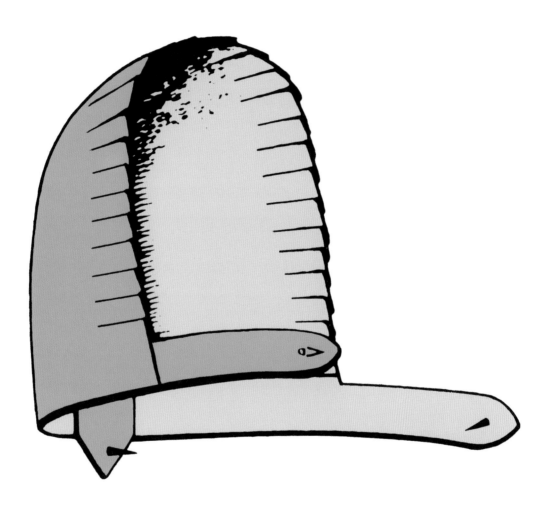

1. a fireproof chef's hat
2. a bowl cover
3. an onion-and-tomato holder for slicing
4. a grapefruit shield
5. a watermelon preserver

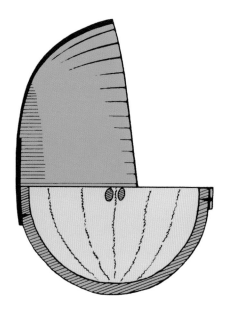

GRAPEFRUIT SHIELD There will be no more annoying jets of juice in the eye with Joseph Fallek's 1928 grapefruit shield. The needles could be stuck into the skin of the fruit to secure it in place. When a spoon was dug into the fruit, the cover stopped the juice before it could hit anyone. To increase the possibility that a large corporation might want to manufacture this as a promotional giveaway, the inventor stated that advertising could be printed on the outside of the shield. You could have a safe, squirt-free breakfast and read at the same time!

The idea of a perfect grapefruit shield has intrigued many inventors. In 1919, Joseph Gibson invented an awkward apparatus that looks more like a lock than a *fruit-eating shield*. And in 1975, Jack Orenstein introduced this space-age *antisplatter device*.

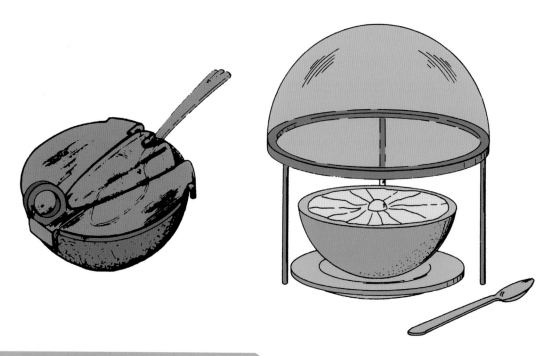

Household Odds and Ends

While inventors have spent a lot of time developing kitchen appliances, they haven't totally neglected the home's other rooms. The following patents were meant to make life just a little more comfortable and uncomplicated.

This 1923 invention was not only shaped like a gun, it was meant to be shot at something.

1. an electric burglar stunner
2. a toy gun
3. a flyswatter
4. a TV channel changer

Reva Harris Keston's 1949 invention was made of inexpensive cardboard so anyone could own one or more of them. It was designed to hold a particular item and helped solve some sticky problems.

1. a ring holder
2. a glazed-doughnut holder
3. a carrying box for onion rings
4. a used-gum receptacle

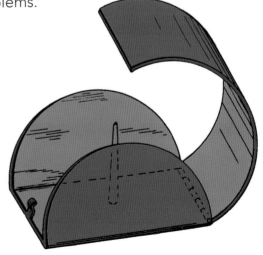

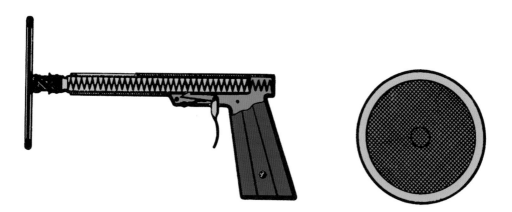

FLYSWATTER George Blake hoped his flyswatter would help solve the problem of pesky flies once and for all. The flat rubber head was attached to a stick called a shaft. When the trigger was pulled, a coiled spring pushed the shaft and rubber head into the air. If the user aimed carefully, there would be one less fly in the world.

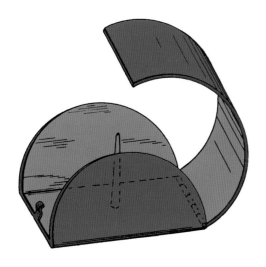

USED-GUM RECEPTACLE Reva Harris Keston invented this used-gum receptacle for two reasons. First, anyone who wanted to save a favorite hunk of gum for one more day's use had a clean place to store it. Second, instead of throwing away gum and having it stick to the sides of the wastepaper basket, this device guaranteed a neat disposal. The invention began as an easy-to-store piece of flat cardboard. The user would bend the thin metal point straight up and place the gum on it. It was then very easy to fold the cardboard along dotted lines until the container was formed. There was even a slit to fasten the flap shut.

When Sidney Palmer and Charles Coventry had this patented in 1854, it was a vast improvement on the old method it replaced. The tub held a liquid and the handle was turned to stir it up. The result: a weekly household chore was made a little easier.

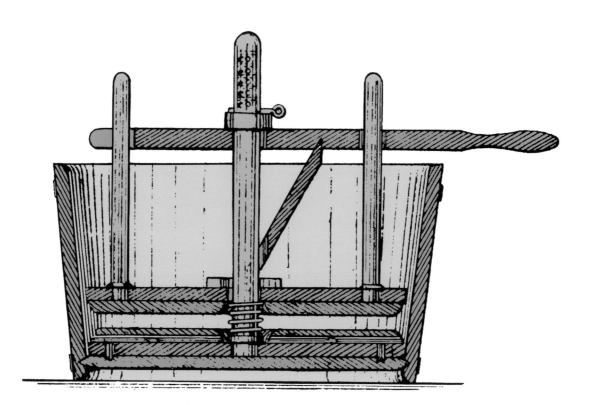

1. an ice-cream maker
2. a washing machine
3. a Swiss-cheese mold
4. a paint mixer

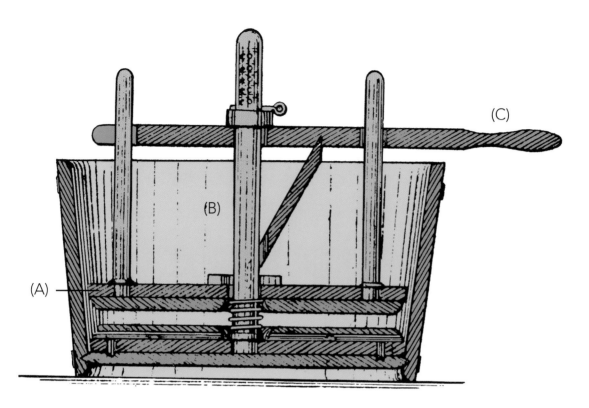

(C)

(B)

(A)

WASHING MACHINE Prior to the patenting of Palmer and Coventry's hand-operated washing machine, clothes had to be cleaned on a scrubbing board. Using a scrubbing board meant that clothes were washed individually and that the washer's hands were in harsh, soapy water for a long time. The washing machine changed all that.

The tub of this model was filled half to three-quarters full with hot water, and soap was added. The washing platform (A) fitted onto a vertical bar (B) that did not move at all. The platform could be raised or lowered with the help of the spring at the base of the vertical bar. When wash was being done, the platform was locked into the lowest position, so all the clothes would be under water. By pulling the handle back and forth, the washing blade (C) churned up the water and clothes—and hopefully cleaned the dirty wash. When the clothes were thoroughly clean, the platform was raised out of the water and the clothes could drain. This machine allowed an entire load of clothes to be washed at the same time.

Operating this washing machine was not very much fun. The weight of the water and clothes required a strong arm to turn the handle.

This ordinary swing was attached by wooden and metal arms to a large box with a small platform next to it. Julius Restein thought up this invention in 1888 to make some unpleasant chores a little easier.

1. a sewing machine
2. a device for sawing, stacking, and counting logs
3. a device for operating a washing machine
4. a weighing scale for people and farm animals

A Greely's 1813 patent was made out of metal and had a little door that could be closed securely. The handle enabled a person to carry it to any room, where it was intended to make winter nights a little more pleasant.

1. a portable mousetrap
2. a foot warmer
3. a sandwich oven
4. a coin-collection box

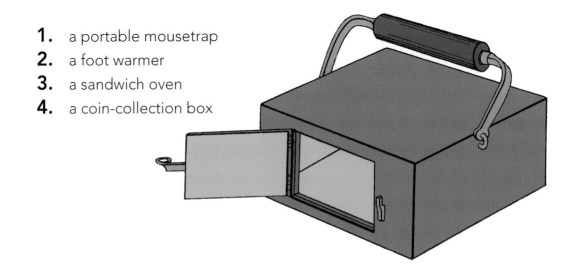

DEVICE FOR OPERATING A WASHING MACHINE

The development of the washing machine made cleaning clothes less time consuming. However, because it had to be operated by hand, the machine was very tiring to run. Julius Restein decided to use the motion of a swing to operate it.

As the swing went back and forth, the motion was carried through two wooden bars. A metal fork transferred this motion to a long rod mounted on the large box next to the swing. The washing machine was placed on the small platform and its handle was attached to the long rod. The rod's back-and-forth movement turned the cleaning blades of the washing machine.

To widen the usefulness of his invention, Restein said that it could operate many other appliances as well, from churns to water pumps to fans. The only requirement was that each appliance had to be designed to run with a back-and-forth motion.

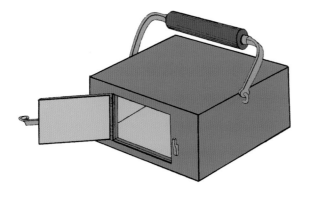

FOOT WARMER

Because the fireplace was still the main source of heat in 1813, many areas in the house were always chilly. To help warm up a small area, A. Greely invented this foot warmer. Hot embers from the fireplace were shoveled into the foot warmer and the door was clicked shut. The embers would stay hot for many hours and the metal box prevented them from starting an accidental fire. The user could read a ghost story long into the night with toasty warm feet.

Down on the Farm

In 1800, 5,300,000 people lived in what was then the United States. By 1860, the population had increased to 39,900,000. This was the result of the opening up of new land in the West for settlement and the immigration to America of northern Europeans seeking political and economic stability. While most people still lived in rural areas, the urban centers, with their promise of well-paying jobs, were growing at an astounding rate. More and more food had to be shipped into the cities—and this demand called for increased agricultural productivity. Inventors responded to this need, and this section shows just a few of the helpful gadgets they thought up for use on the farm.

This 1903 invention was made of metal and thick glass and could be adjusted to fit any size or shape head. When on, it protected the wearer from injury.

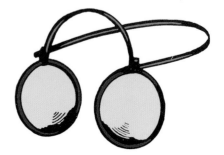

1. a pair of adjustable sunglasses
2. an earmuff device
3. an eye protector for chickens
4. a device to collect heat from the sun to warm the head

This gadget was fastened to the farmer's boot and speeded up a routine farm chore.

1. a foot seeder
2. a water-locating device
3. an insecticide spray
4. an automatic fertilizer-and-soil tester

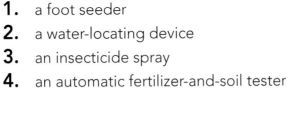

EYE PROTECTOR FOR CHICKENS

Chickens are generally very nasty birds, pecking at anything that annoys them or interferes with their feeding. Housing hundreds of chickens in a large coop meant that numerous fights would occur each day. So Andrew Jackson, Jr., invented this eye protector for chickens, hoping to save many birds from being blinded or killed. The device was worn just like an ordinary pair of glasses, and a special feature allowed the farmer to adjust the glasses to fit any size or type of chicken.

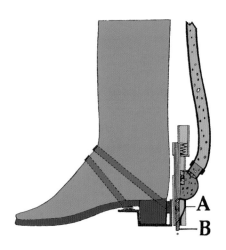

FOOT SEEDER
in an attempt to increase the amount of land that could be planted, farmers turned to machines for help. One of them was this 1856 foot seeder by G. A. Meacham. The device was strapped to the farmer's work boot and a hose connected it to a container of seed which the farmer carried on his back.

When the farmer set his foot into the soil, a number of things happened: the tubular part (A) was pushed upward while the seed channel (B) dug a small hole. The upward motion of the tubular part opened a tiny door that dropped the seed down the seed channel and into the hole. At the same time a scoop put the correct amount of seed in position for the next "planting step."

While foot seeders were developed and perfected by many inventors, their usefulness faded as farms became larger and more commercial. It was not long before the processes of plowing and planting were combined in a single operation, at first with horse-drawn machines and later with self-propelled vehicles.

Something produced on a farm was placed inside the oval cups, and, when the handle was turned, the cups spun around and performed an early morning farm chore.

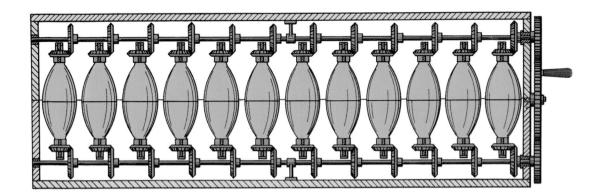

1. a milk pasteurizer
2. a potato peeler
3. an egg cleaner

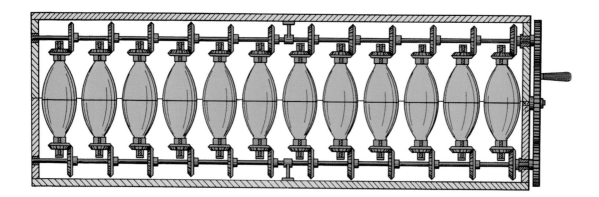

EGG CLEANER In order to make eggs look nice at the market (and ensure that they were sold), the pre-dawn collection of eggs was followed by monotonous hand cleaning to remove unsightly smudges and dirt. Alton H. Wilde's 1937 egg cleaner was an early attempt to automate the procedure. Each egg was placed in a cup lined with scrubbing material. When the lid was closed and locked, the eggs were surrounded by the material. The handle turned each egg cup and the scrubbing material—and in a few seconds, the eggs were clean. The machine could be made with as many egg cups as the farmer wanted, and if further speed seemed necessary, a motor could be attached to the handle.

Today, when a chicken lays an egg, it is caught in a chute and deposited on a conveyor belt. The conveyor belt whisks the eggs through a cleaning spray, separates them according to size, and deposits them in the containers. An egg hardly has a chance to get dirty.

This short wooden chair had straps that buckled on so that it could be carried about with ease. When in use, it ensured that the user was at just the right height for work.

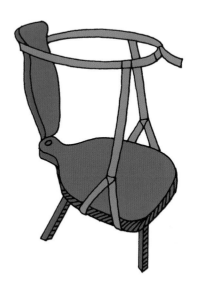

1. a toilet seat for farm animals
2. a baby's chair
3. a milking stool

Patented in 1879, this invention had a large steam engine to run it and was an attempt to automate something usually done by horses.

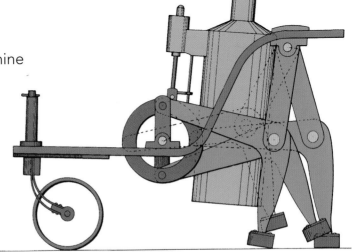

1. a corn-husking machine
2. a traction engine
3. a washing machine
4. a peanut roaster

MILKING STOOL

In 1887, Allen Cowen patented this milking stool. As the illustration shows, it was worn around the waist and provided the milkmaid with an instant seat. It was just the right height for milking, and the hinged back made movement in any direction possible. And, of course, because the milkmaid didn't have to constantly tend to her chair when moving, this not only saved energy but was also a way to speed up work.

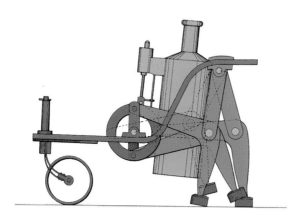

TRACTION ENGINE

Plows or wagons and other farming machines were usually pulled by teams of horses. J. Praul's traction engine was an early type of tractor. The curious feature of this invention was that instead of turning wheels, the steam engine helped four metal feet to take forward steps. Many of the first attempts to make self-propelled vehicles are remarkable because the inventors consciously attempted to imitate the way humans or animals moved. This traction engine might have reminded many people who saw it of a giant hissing cow or a team of workhorses.

If you think this is a cow, you're partially correct. It was shaped like a cow, was made of a heavy material, and had a very specific, though hopefully not too obvious, use on the farm.

1. an inflatable mooing scarecrow
2. a hunting decoy
3. a set of insulated underwear for cows

HUNTING DECOY Mr. John Sievers, Jr., invented his hunting decoy in 1897 to help hunters bag ducks, geese, and other game birds. The hunters would climb into the cow suit and pull the solidly formed head and the cloth flaps closed. They could then roam the fields like any other cow and fool a flock of passing birds into landing nearby. There were holes in various parts of the costume for viewing the terrain and sky and, judging by the size of the cow, plenty of extra room to store a hearty lunch.

Getting Around

This section contains a few of the attempts made to help people or things move from one place to another. Some got their energy from nature, some used steam engines, and some were run by hand. However they were run, they all demonstrate the desire of inventors to improve the ways of getting around.

This is part of an entire system developed by George Owen in 1901 that would pick up an item and deliver it quickly.

1. a hot pizza-pie transporter
2. an automatic letter carrier
3. a grocery, medicine, and small-package delivery system

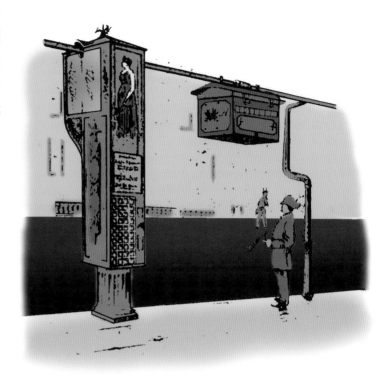

This side view shows only three of this grasshopper's six steel legs. The body of the grasshopper was made of cloth or leather and, with some help, it could move around.

1. an automatic, movable lure for bugs, frogs, and small rodents
2. a jumping shoe
3. a plane with fold-away wings
4. a houseboat

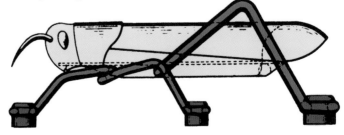

AUTOMATIC LETTER CARRIER This was George Owen's idea for a completely automatic letter carrier. A person would deposit a letter in the curbside box pictured. The letter was lifted up automatically and deposited in the waiting box conveyors, which would then whisk it and other letters collected off to the central post office for sorting. The sorted letters would then be loaded back into the conveyors for delivery. When a letter arrived for an individual, a signal would be given at his home and he would stop by the local mailbox to pick it up. Unfortunately, the cost of setting up this system and the number of possible mechanical problems worked against the adoption of this invention.

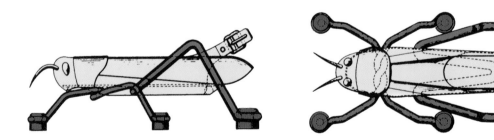

JUMPING SHOES George and May Southgate designed these jumping shoes in 1922 to encourage children to run and jump. The boy or girl wore these over ordinary shoes or sneakers and a buckle held them in place. The six steel legs were very strong and springy. When a child tried to jump, the legs would allow the child to jump farther than was normally possible. Each leg had a rubber pad on the bottom which softened the landings and helped the wearer to avoid injuries.

N o, this isn't a stove on stilts. This 1868 invention had a steam engine in it that helped it to move. Once in motion, the inventor hoped it would be an efficient and speedy way to carry things.

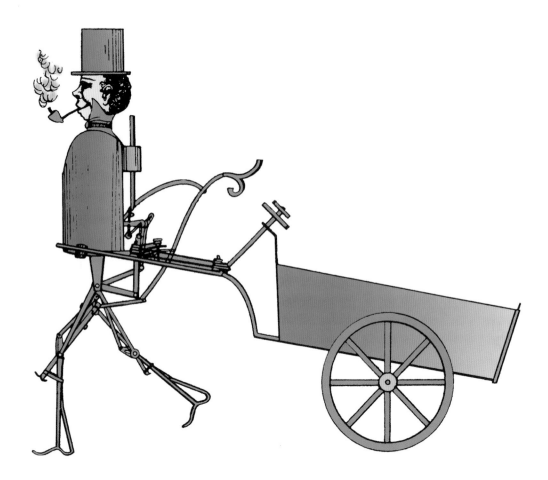

1. a steam carriage
2. an early rocket ship
3. a deep-sea diving suit

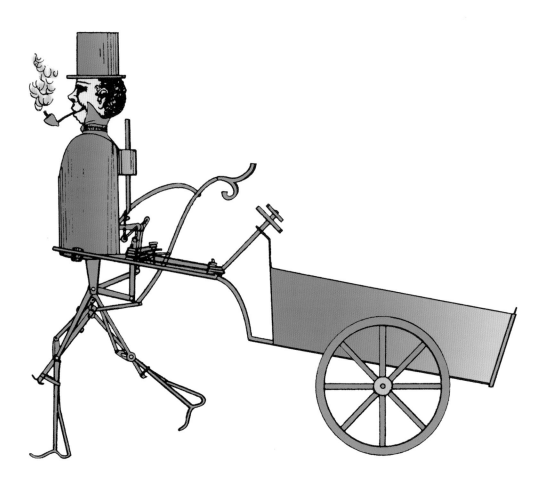

STEAM CARRIAGE It is very possible that Zador Drederick and Isaac Grass, the co-inventors of this steam carriage, were having fun when they made it look like an iron man. The chest contained a steam engine, and the head and tall top hat were designed to let smoke and excess steam escape. The engine and head were placed on top of two metal legs which were moved by the engine and could actually take forward steps. This mechanical man pulled a two-wheeled cart. The driver sat in the cart and could control the size of the steps the metal man took and make the machine step over any large rocks that might be in the road. Since the steam engine was very small, it couldn't be operated for long periods of time without frequent stops to refuel. Because it was much more practical for hauling things over short distances, the inventors hoped it would prove to be a speedy way to deliver small packages in the crowded city streets.

John Cook's invention captured the wind in giant canvas sails and let it do the work.

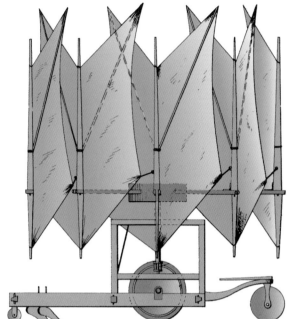

1. a multi-sailed racing boat
2. a wind engine
3. a water pump
4. a helicopter

This simple, straightforward 1884 patent will get you from one place to another in comfort.

1. a roller skate with springs
2. a baby carriage
3. a shoe for injured individuals

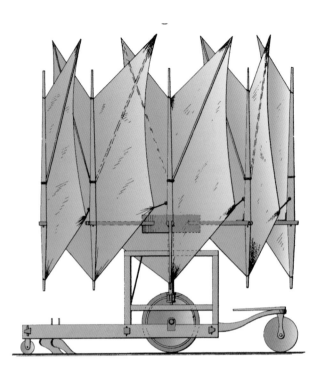

WIND ENGINE John Cook's 1878 wind engine looks complicated, but actually the way it worked was very simple. Eight sails were attached to a giant horizontal wheel structure in a circular pattern. When the wind hit the sails, the wheel began to turn. The energy created by the spinning wheel was transferred by a gear to the large wheels at the center of the machine. These wheels, which touched the ground, pushed the entire wind engine forward. The driver sat behind the small wheel at the right, and a stick allowed him to steer the machine. This invention could be used to pull a wagon or a plow or simply to carry people.

BABY CARRIAGE George Clark designed this baby carriage as a very fancy high-top shoe, complete with laces and an umbrella to keep rain or sun off baby's head. The inventor hoped that wealthy parents would prefer to have their children pushed around town in this unusual novelty carriage instead of the kind that most other people had.

This 1889 invention looked like two giant wings and a tail and had a large helium balloon attached to it. With some effort, it was supposed to get into the air, but for what purpose?

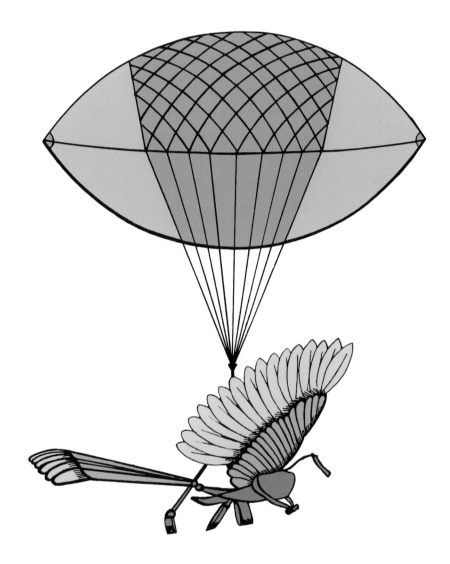

1. a flying machine
2. a life preserver
3. a weather-forecasting balloon

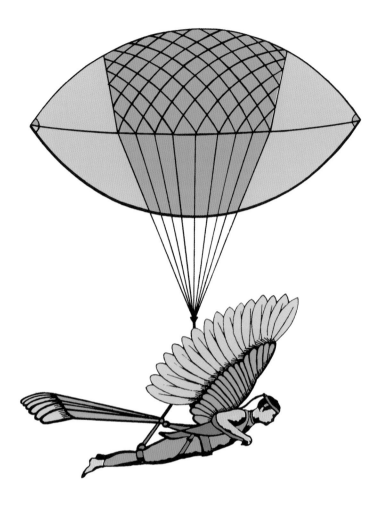

FLYING MACHINE Mr. Reuben Jasper Spalding expected his balloon and feathered wings and tail flying machine would make him the first person to achieve independent flight. The user actually wore the wings and tail like a suit. When the person's arms and legs moved, the wings and tail would also move. Mr. Spalding calculated that by flapping the wings up and down as a bird does, the wearer would be able to soar into the air. The balloon was attached to the back of the invention to make it and the user lighter and thus easier to get off the ground. Spalding was not alone in this quest to imitate the flight of birds. Hundreds of tinkers throughout the United States developed similar (and equally unsuccessful) flying machines. The major problem with all of these inventions was that in order to lift a person the wings had to be very large and heavy. No one could flap them hard enough or long enough to lift himself off the ground.

Self - Improvement Whether You Want to or Not

Hundreds of books are published every year to help us be better cooks, car mechanics, or gardeners. Schools offer courses on self-awareness or filmmaking or quilting. We are living in a time of organized self-improvement. Yet, as the following section shows, inventors have always had our best interests in mind.

This machine was made of metal and had parts that moved. In order to use this, a person had to be securely strapped to it. Once in place, it would help the users do something they couldn't do before.

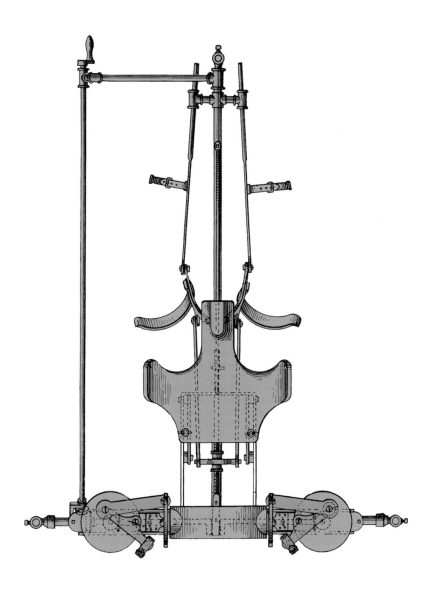

1. a back brace
2. a weight-reducing machine
3. a bathing device for animals
4. a swimming teacher

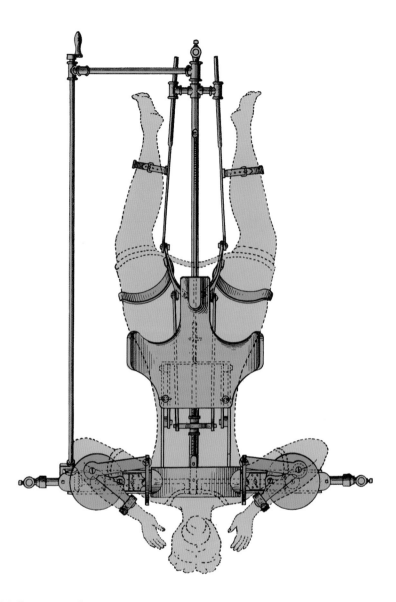

SWIMMING TEACHER First, James Emerson's 1896 swimming teacher was placed in shallow water. Next, the person who wished to learn to swim was strapped into the machine—with the entire body, except for the head, below water. The machine held the person up in the water and allowed the arms and legs to move only in the correct motion for swimming. An instructor would teach the student how to turn his or her head while swimming in order to breathe, as well as the proper pace for leg and arm movement. The inventor felt the swimming teacher would be particularly useful at camps where one instructor could watch over five, ten, or more students at the same time.

S Anderson's 1897 implement looks like a horse's bit and was in fact used in the mouth.

1. a policeman's whistle
2. a bad-breath tester
3. a harmonica
4. a mouthpiece for preventing snoring

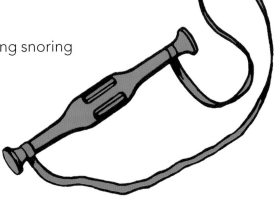

M ade of lightweight metal, this 1899 invention was placed inside the mouth and was supposed to help the user overcome a problem.

1. a breathing aid
2. a teeth straightener
3. a device for aiding cure of stammering

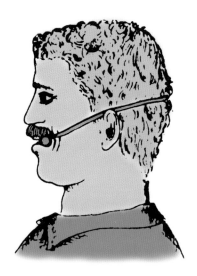

MOUTHPIECE FOR PREVENTING SNORING

S. Anderson's mouthpiece for preventing snoring was placed in the mouth just before bedtime. The strap held it there securely even when the user was sound asleep. The mouthpiece had four tiny openings in it which allowed air to go into and out of the sleeper's mouth easily. Mr. Anderson believed that because his invention kept the user's mouth open, air would not collect in the throat and force its way out, causing the snoring sound.

DEVICE FOR AIDING CURE OF STAMMERING

R. B. G. Gardner's device for aiding cure of stammering was a mouthful to say and a mouthful to use as well. It went into the patient's mouth, and the two grids went around the tongue. Once in position, the device limited the way the mouth and tongue moved and forced the stammerer to pronounce words distinctly and without pauses. Gardner did not expect the patient to wear the uncomfortable device all of the time. But, he insisted, regular practice with it would get the user accustomed to speaking correctly.

T his curious device would be one of the first things to greet you in the morning. It ensured a prompt beginning to each day.

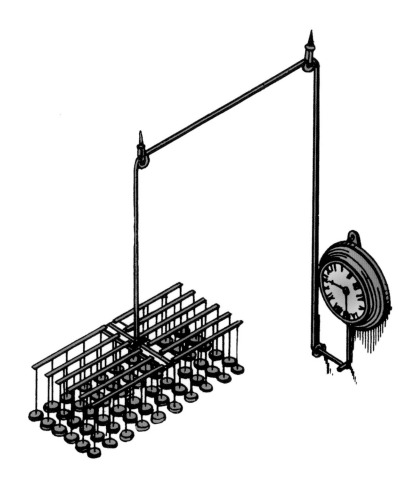

1. a device for drying and storing socks
2. a device for waking people from sleep
3. a measuring and weighing apparatus
4. an automatic lamp
5. a chiming toy

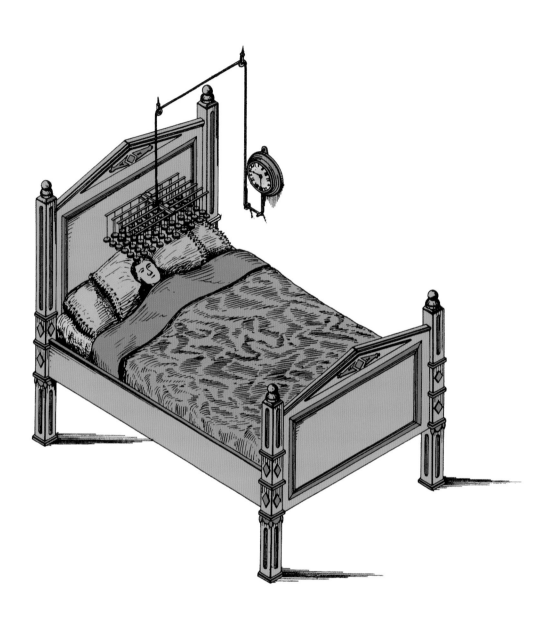

DEVICE FOR WAKING PEOPLE FROM SLEEP Samuel Applegate wanted to make sure that everyone got up on time, so in 1882 he invented this device for waking people from sleep. Sixty corks were attached to individual pieces of string and all of them were hung above the sleeping person by a cord which ran from the invention to a clock. The clock would signal the time to wake up by releasing the cord and dropping the sixty corks on the unsuspecting sleeper. To widen his invention's usefulness, Mr. Applegate also explained that it could turn on the gas heater or be used as a burglar alarm.

This 1956 invention could be made out of cloth or plastic, and, when worn properly, it prevented messy mishaps.

1. a bird diaper
2. a harness to limit the movement of toddlers
3. a finger brace
4. a sleeping cap

George Jorgenson's invention could be held in the hand and was easy to use. The inventor hoped it would correct family problems simply and thus be a big sales hit.

1. a hand-held mirror with battery-operated light
2. a frying pan with built-in timer
3. a spanking paddle

BIRD DIAPER To ensure a spotless house, Bertha Dlugi invented the bird diaper. The pet's owner would gently slip the bird's feet and wings into the diaper and secure it with a tiny clasp. The bird's legs and wings could move, so the bird was free to fly or hop as usual. At the tail end a tiny cloth patch acted as a diaper, catching excrement before it fell to the floor. The diaper could be made in different sizes, so any type of bird could be fitted with one.

SPANKING PADDLE George Jorgenson invented this modern spanking paddle in 1953. He made the paddle part big enough to cover "a substantial area of the rump of a child." Since the inventor didn't want his invention to injure the child, he provided a safety feature—the handle of the spanker would collapse if the swat was too hard.

If you say this is a suitcase, you're partially correct. However, when opened up, it became something else.

1. a bed
2. a table
3. a portmanteau and bathtub
4. a tent

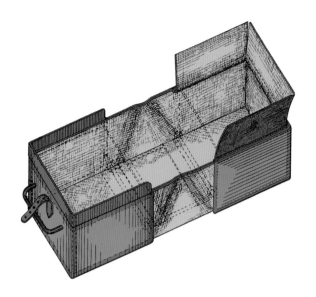

A PORTMANTEAU AND BATHTUB Ethelbert Watts invented this portmanteau and bathtub in 1876 to ensure that a traveler would always be able to relax in a warm tub of water. The canvas bag could be used to carry clothes while traveling. When a stop was made, however, it could be opened up into a small bathtub, complete with a back rest. Hopefully, the tub would be dry before it was time to pack up the clothes again.

Many people have worked variations on the portable bathtub idea. A. Seligsberg's tiny satchel, invented in 1876, opened up into a tub, also with an elevated back rest. And in 1977, Susan Younker developed this inflatable rubber tub for use in places where only a shower stall is available.

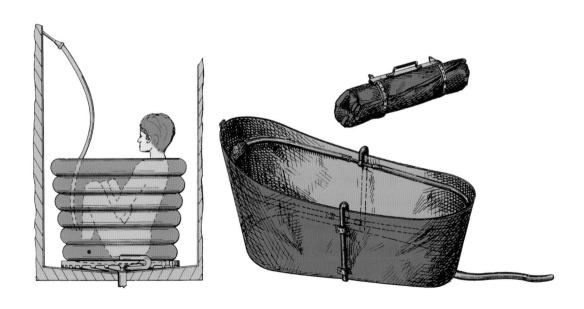

art of Isidor Keller's 1884 invention was made of metal and could be bolted in one spot. The other part had two leather straps that held something in place. The entire device worked to correct a sloppy situation.

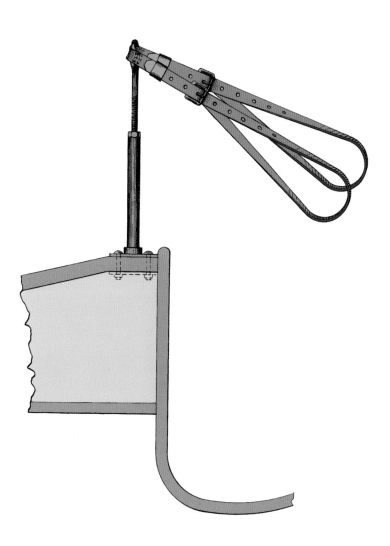

1. a scholar's shoulder brace
2. a horse harness
3. an exercise machine
4. a device to hold sheep for shearing

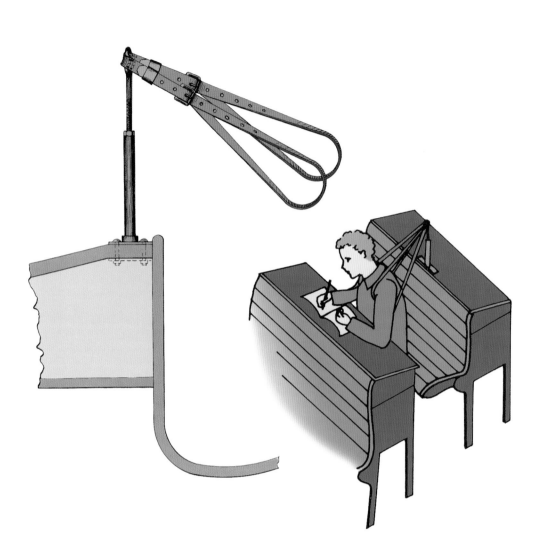

SCHOLAR'S SHOULDER BRACE if the teacher's watchful eyes couldn't keep students alert, Isidor Keller's scholar's shoulder brace could. The student would put one strap around each shoulder. These would force the wearer to sit up straight. Mr. Keller claimed that this position was the best one in which to learn proper penmanship.

One Thing Leads to Another

This section is completely different from the other seven. It is divided into two parts and each part begins with a very simple invention. One of the inventions is an early type of bicycle called a *velocipede;* the other is a bellows. From these uncomplicated, simple beginnings you'll see some of the changes and developments inventors made.

These are by no means all of the different patents for bicycles and bellows. For two-wheeled bicycles alone, hundreds of designs have been patented over the years. What you will see is a carefully chosen selection that highlights the interesting and odd stages these inventions went through.

At first glance this appears to be a toy horse on wheels. Actually it is an early form of bicycle, known as a *velocipede* (which in French means "swift-footed"), that Harvey Reynolds invented in 1866. A front view reveals a stirrup and crank hookup which the rider pedaled with his or her legs. The steering was controlled by the bridle lines that ran from the horse's mouth to the rear wheels. Mr. Reynolds's velocipede was a deluxe model, intended for use by children with parents who could afford the special craftsmanship required to construct it.

Most velocipedes were much more simply designed and were meant to be ridden by adults as well as children. They were usually shaped like large tricycles. There was one wheel in front with a handlebar for steering and two wheels in the back with a foot crank. But many variations developed. Some models had two wheels in the front, one in the back. Some had pedals on the front wheel (or wheels), some were operated by hand and not by foot. One 1878 model, designed especially for females, came with a sidesaddle and suspended stirrup.

The velocipede was very popular, in part because the three wheels meant anyone could ride it. But soon two-wheeled bicycles began to appear in greater numbers. They would slowly replace the three-wheeled velocipede because they were lighter, went faster, and were easier to store. The *improved bicycle* pictured was patented in 1883 by William Klahr. It was propelled by a combination of pedals and a ratchet wheel. The rear wheel is much larger than the front wheel because, inventors reasoned, if one turn of an ordinary-size wheel covered a certain number of feet, a larger wheel would cover that many more. This meant that for every turn of the pedal, the rider would cover more ground. Again, many variations developed, the large front wheel with pedals being the most popular.

John Lose took the concept of the enlarged wheel to its extreme in his 1885 *one-wheeled vehicle.* The rider sat inside the giant wheel and made it roll forward by pedaling with his feet. While this couldn't be steered like an ordinary velocipede or bicycle, it did have a short handle that allowed the rider to "direct" the machine by pulling and leaning in the direction he wanted to go. This illustration shows a rather cheery and carefree rider, so relaxed he could take the time to smoke a cigar. Once one of these machines got rolling, however, it would be very difficult to control it—or stop it, for that matter. Lose designed his vehicle for long-distance traveling and probably hoped that on the open road there wouldn't be too much traffic to contend with.

If Lose's giant wheel was for long journeys, Louis Schutte's 1899 *monocycle* was better suited for local travel. It had a pedal and gear arrangement that transferred leg energy into wheel movement and a handle to aid in maneuvering. Once again, the illustration tries to show that riding this vehicle would be easy. In fact, it takes a great deal of skill and practice to balance and control a monocycle.

All of these different forms of wheeled transportation were being improved and modified at the same time. While one inventor was perfecting a two-wheeled bicycle, another was at work on a one-wheeled version, while someone else was trying to improve the three-wheeled model. They were all trying to create a form of transportation that people would want to buy because it was lighter or faster than the one they already had, was easier to store, or seemed better suited to their particular needs. Eventually, the two-wheeled bicycle became the most popular, now being made of light metal, with up to ten racing gears and hand brakes. The velocipede became known as a tricycle and is used by children who haven't learned to balance on a two-wheeler. And the monocycle, now better known as a unicyle, is the rarest of all, being ridden by the few people who can master the necessary skills.

And yet, there was still one more interesting development in store for wheeled vehicles.

While all these one-, two-, and three-wheeled machines were being perfected, someone invented a small, portable source of power, the gas engine. It wasn't long before engines began powering anything with wheels, including monocycles. Edwin Himes's 1911 *motorcycle* was not the first two-wheeled motorcycle invented, but it is interesting to study anyway. His design combined elements from three different types of transportation. The two big seats, the wide floor, and the cabinet space were features more often found in horse-drawn carriages. The frame, with its two wheels and handlebars, was from the bicycle. And, finally, there was the modern source of power, the engine concealed under the rear seat. It wouldn't be long before the carriage disappeared from general use, the bicycle was ridden more for recreation than for everyday travel or for carrying goods, and the gas engine began to power cars, trucks, planes, and buses.

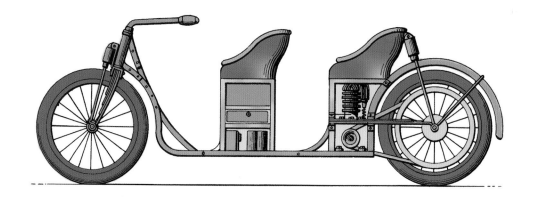

Inventors love to improve and develop an original notion. Here, for instance, is John Grennell's 1838 patent for a bellows. The operation of a bellows is not complicated. A leather or canvas bag with one small opening in it is attached to two pieces of wood shaped something like paddles. The hole of the bag goes at the wide end of the paddles, and the paddles

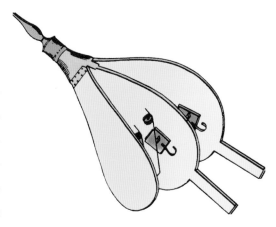

are joined there by a hinge. When the paddles are pushed together by hand, air is forced through the opening. Bellows were, and still are, used to relight wood or coal fires that have died down because of a lack of air.

Since bellows had been in use for hundreds of years, Grennell was not patenting the concept of the bellows. Since all that remains of his patent application is this drawing, it is hard to say definitely what he was claiming as original. Most likely he wanted to patent the springlike feature which would automatically open the paddles up after each use.

Twenty-six years later, in 1864, Henry Neumeyer patented his version of an improved bellows. Neumeyer believed that a good pair of feet could compress the air bag much more effectively. The hose was positioned near the fire and the operator pumped with only one foot. This bellows was not intended for small home fires, however. It was designed for a blacksmith's shop. The smith could pump the bellows and still have both hands free to work.

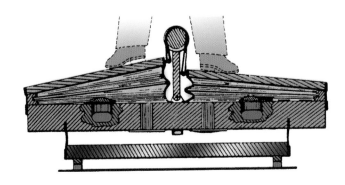

Another improvement made on the bellows is shown in this drawing of George Peek's 1870 *bellows*. A metal arm allowed the user to stand away from the hot fire and still be able to pump air into the embers. Once again, this bellows was intended for large furnaces, such as those used by glass manufacturers.

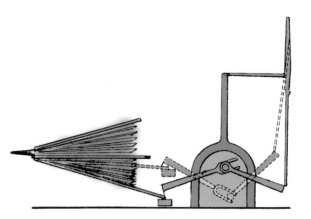

In the course of the development of the bellows, someone came to the conclusion (or, more likely, accidentally discovered) that if the leather bag could push out air, it could suck it in as well, and in so doing, draw in dirt and dust. This invention was first referred to as a pumping machine but has come to be called a vacuum cleaner.

This 1909 *vacuum cleaning device* was designed by C. J. Harvey. It was operated just like a large hand bellows. The machine could be wheeled to the area that was going to be cleaned. Once it was put in position, the operator got onto a small platform, which anchored the machine in place, and began pumping the handle with one hand. The other hand moved the collecting nozzle in as wide an arc as possible. When one area was clean, the whole apparatus was then moved to the next dusty spot.

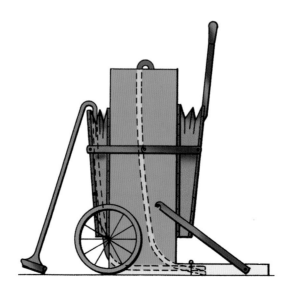

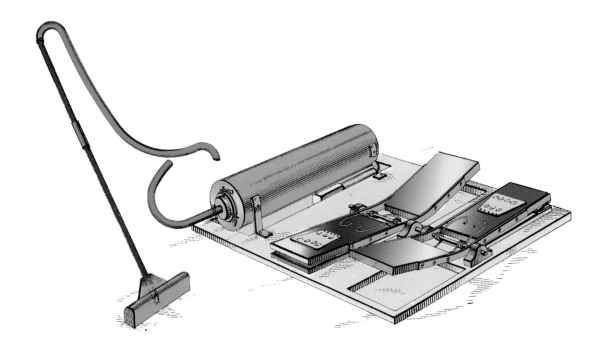

If a foot-operated bellows was better, the same must be true for a vacuum cleaner. Charles Wickwire's *pumping mechanism* of 1910 had two sets of pumping pedals, no doubt to double the cleaning power of the machine. It was designed for professional rug cleaners and not for everyday home use.

So far we've seen (1) the simple bellows principle converted to a vacuum, (2) hand operation give way to foot power, and (3) the use of extension nozzles to increase the area that could be cleaned. Unfortunately, the vacuum cleaning machines were still inconvenient. The nozzles could only be six or eight feet long because they began to lose their suction power if they were any longer. Also, it was hard for one person to pump and move a long hose around at the same time. This meant these machines had to be moved and set up several times just to clean one room.

Then, in 1912, Alexander Jack hit upon the perfect answer to increase mobility without a loss of power. Jack simply had the operator wear his portable *air-withdrawing or vacuum-producing apparatus.* The operator could walk to the area to be cleaned and at the same time create the pull necessary to clean it up.

As with the bicycle, the hand– or foot-operated vacuum cleaner would change completely when a source of portable power was developed. The use of small electric motors to operate the bellows led to the development of the vacuum cleaner we are familiar with today.

Afterword

This book has presented some very unusual inventions—a vacuum cleaner attached to the feet, a dimple maker, and a steam carriage in the shape of a man, to name just three. Yet as oddly varied as these and all of the other inventions are, they have something in common: the inventor of each one had it patented. What is a patent anyway?

Quite simply, a patent is a grant issued by the federal government that gives an inventor the "exclusive right" to his or her discovery for seventeen years in the United States and its territories. In effect, the inventor alone decides who can and cannot make, use, or sell his invention.

But why patent some of these strange inventions? Who would possibly want them? The answer is that you can never tell what might or might not intrigue people, what might turn out to be valuable at some later date. Recently, a man took a small, smooth rock, put it into a cardboard box, and called it a Pet Rock. It had to be one of the all-time silly ideas, and yet, in less than a year he sold over 500,000 of them. Then there is the story of Joseph Henry, who decided *not* to take out a patent on his discovery.

Joseph Henry was a teacher of science at Albany Academy when he made his remarkable discovery in 1831. After much research, he found a way to transmit electric current through great lengths of wire and, in effect, invented the first practical telegraph. But Henry never took out a patent on his invention. He felt, he said later, that it was not "compatible with the dignity of science to confine benefits which might be derived from it to the exclusive right of any individual."

Six years later, Samuel F. B. Morse took Henry's findings (and those of others working in the field), improved on them, built his own telegraph—and patented it! Watching Morse's fortune and fame grow, Henry's only comment on his obvious mistake was: "I was perhaps too fastidious."

In a society that holds the shrewd and successful individual in such high esteem, most people would consider Joseph Henry an idealistic fool. And in truth, Henry was probably overreacting to the legal jargon of the patent law and to the possibility that some bit of new knowledge could be withheld from the world.

A patent *does* give an inventor sole control over the invention. At the same time, though, it puts the invention on display to the public. Anyone who so wishes can study the patents housed in the Patent Search Room (in Arlington, Virginia) or in one of the more than twenty regional libraries that have printed volumes of patents. What is more, a patent includes no rule on how an inventor must sell or use the rights to an invention. If Joseph Henry had obtained a patent, he could have let anyone use his discovery free of charge.

Today, the preparation and execution of a patent application is an extremely complex operation. To ensure that it is carried out properly, almost everyone connected with patents (including the Patent and Trademark Office itself) recommends that a lawyer with a knowledge of the requirements and procedures for getting a patent be hired to do the paperwork. And there can be a lot of paperwork. In 1969, Gene Amdahl and his fifteen co-inventors were granted a patent that consisted of 495 sheets of drawings and 469 sheets of specifications.

An application for a patent is complex, in part to lessen the number of silly claims, but largely to ensure that what is patented *is* really new. There is an application fee of $65, plus additional costs, depending on the length of the application. A detailed description of how to make and use the invention must be given; if it is an improvement on an existing invention, the ways in which it differs must be specified. While a scale model of the invention is usually not required, when possible a drawing of the invention, or all of its new features, must be included. The drawing can be done by the inventor, but usually an artist trained in patent drawings will be hired for this. After all these steps are completed, the Patent Office examines the application to be sure it has been filled out correctly. Then the Patent Office conducts a "search," or examines all similar registered patents, to ensure that what is to be patented is really original. When accepted, there is a $100 issue fee, plus charges for printing the specifications and drawings.

All of these steps in getting a patent may sound complicated. Yet, many people must find the time and expense worthwhile in some way, since on an average over 103,000 patent applications are made each year. Thomas Edison found the whole process so rewarding that he obtained 1,093 patents, a record number. Despite the legal and financial requirements and complications, approximately 25 percent of all patents are issued to individuals not connected with corporations or research institutions.

Robert Patch is one of them. In 1963, he was granted patent number 3,091,888 for his *toy truck* invention. As the illustration shows, the truck came apart completely and could be put together in a number of different ways. The specification sheet for this truck claims it can be "readily assembled and disassembled by a child," The statement must be true, since Robert Patch was five years old when he invented it.

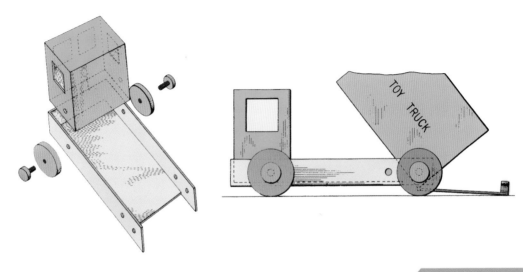

From silly to sublime, from the practical to the frivolous, the range of things invented is incredible and amazing. All that is required is a spark of imagination, a little fiddling and thinking, and, who knows, you may just invent something as important as Walter Hunt's little safety pin.